CW01465306

Original title:

My Heart, Your Heart

Author: William Harris

ISBN HARDBACK: 978-9908-0-0482-2

ISBN PAPERBACK: 978-9908-0-0483-9

A Radiant Tangle

In a world of ups and downs,
You stole my sock, I wore your crown.
Our laughter echoed, silly and loud,
Two clowns together, a whimsical crowd.

Chasing rainbows, tripping on air,
You punched my arm, but I didn't care.
We danced like noodles, flopping around,
With every giggle, love we found.

Your jokes are treasures, quirky and bright,
I fell off the chair, what a sight!
With each silly prank, our bond grows tight,
Like two tangled kites, soaring in flight.

So let's skip through puddles, jump in the breeze,
You bring the humor; I'll bring the cheese.
Together we'll craft this joyous tangle,
Life's grand circus, let's just wrangle.

Harmonies of Togetherness

In the kitchen we both dance,
Spilling flour, taking a chance.
You sing off-key, I join in loud,
We're a goofy, giggling crowd.

Pasta boiling over in a pot,
You claim it's something I've forgot.
But as we laugh and toss the salad,
We find love in this playful ballad.

Silent Conversations

We share a look across the room,
And suddenly there's too much zoom.
A wink, a smile— our secret code,
In crowded silence, love's bestowed.

You steal my fries, I let it slide,
In every bite, my joy can't hide.
In whispered words, the joyful tease,
Our hearts converse with perfect ease.

Pulses of Connection

The way you trip over your shoelace,
Turns a stumble into a race.
We burst with laughter, not a care,
Your clumsiness? A love affair.

With every beat, we share our quirks,
I laugh at all your silly jerks.
Each little fail, a tale that's spun,
In our own rhythm, we have fun.

Dances of Desire

In the living room, we spin and sway,
To tunes that make the boredom stray.
You step on toes, I twirl away,
But laughter holds us in display.

With every move, we jive and dive,
Our silly steps keep love alive.
In this dance, we find our spark,
Two silly hearts that leave a mark.

Passions Interwoven

In a dance of socks, we twirl and spin,
With mismatched colors, let the chaos begin!
Our laughter rings louder than a clanging bell,
Like a two-headed chef cooking chocolate gel.

Bridges of Emotion

We build our towers with blocks of jest,
Playing cards with jokes, we're surely blessed.
A trampoline of puns, we leap so high,
Catching giggles as they bounce through the sky.

Reflections in a Shared Gaze

In the mirror, we pose, looking quite absurd,
Sporting silly hats, oh it's simply heard!
With a wink and a grin, we share our stare,
Like two bewildered owls caught unaware.

A Symphony of Two

In our kitchen band, we play pots and pans,
Conducting our laughter, while dance it scans.
Each note a punchline, as we sing off key,
Creating a melody, just you and me.

Synced in Silence

When your eyes roll, I can't help but grin,
Like two spoons stirring up the same old din.
We laugh at secrets no one else knows,
In our quirky dance, the humor just flows.

A nod, a wink, the joke's on the shelf,
You're the punchline to my own little self.
With silent giggles, we create a scene,
In this world of whispers, we're a fun machine.

Vows in the Vein

In a world of chaos, we made a pact,
A sacred bond, with humor intact.
You wear mismatched socks, I misplace my keys,
Together we stumble, just as it pleases.

A toast to the mess that is our delight,
We'll keep laughing hard, through day and night.
With each silly mishap, we add to our lore,
In this love of ours, who could ask for more?

The Warmth of Us

Sipping cold coffee, we laugh at our fate,
Life's little quirks, oh, they're worth the wait!
Underneath blankets, we share all our dreams,
Like two fuzzy bears, we're just bursting at the seams.

With toast that's burnt and soup that's too hot,
We're culinary geniuses, or maybe not!
Yet in this chaos, the love clearly shows,
As laughter spills out, it just grows and grows.

Threads of Desire

In every mishap, there's a spark that's bright,
Like tangled yarn on a lazy night.
You tug at my patience, I pull at your shoe,
Yet somehow we weave a story anew.

With playful banter and a dash of flair,
We've stitched together quite the love affair.
So here's to the moments that twist and that twine,
In this fabric of joy, you're perfectly mine.

Whispers of Affection

You stole my snack, oh what a thief,
But your smile brings me sweet relief.
We giggle and laugh, a silly pair,
With secret whispers hanging in the air.

Your quirky dance, a sight to see,
I trip and fall, you laugh with glee.
With jest and play, we rule the day,
Two clumsy fools, in love's ballet.

Intertwined Beats

Like mismatched socks, we go astray,
In the jumble of life's awkward play.
A high-five fails, but we don't quit,
We just laugh and call it a perfect fit.

Your goofy face, it cracks me up,
While sipping tea from a tiny cup.
We play hopscotch on the sidewalk, too,
Just two wild hearts, colored in blue.

The Language of Love

When you say 'pasta' with that twang,
I burst out laughing; what a slang!
Your funny way of saying 'hello',
Turns the dullest day into a show.

In the world of awkward hugs we thrive,
Both of us trying, just to survive.
With silly poems that make no sense,
Our laughter forms a sweet pretense.

Chasing Distant Stars

Running after dreams, we trip on shoes,
Your clumsy charm, I just can't lose.
We caper through fields, like wild-eyed kids,
With our own tales and goofy bids.

In a galaxy where penguins dance,
We find ourselves with no second chance.
Together we'll spin, we'll laugh, we'll shout,
Two comedic stars, in love no doubt.

The Language of Affection

In the land of giggles, we play,
Where every word's a funny say.
A wink, a nudge, thumbs-up in cheer,
Our silent codes are crystal clear.

You crack a joke, my laughter bursts,
In your odd ways, joy surely flirts.
With every smile, we share a dance,
Two hearts speaking in a glance.

Ties that Bind

We frolic with puns, no need for rules,
In this merry game, we're the silliest fools.
A tug-of-war with bubble gum strings,
Together we laugh at the silliest things.

With quirks that tie us in laughter's embrace,
Your sock puppets fill our shared space.
From play fights to pranks that always amuse,
Life's a circus when it's just me and you.

Harmonies of Emotion

Our duet of chuckles, it plays on repeat,
And every misstep is a musical feat.
A serenade of silliness fills the air,
With harmonies sweet, we banish despair.

Your quirky dance moves make me lose track,
Together we're off, there's no looking back.
Every giggle a note in our love song,
In this silly symphony, we both belong.

Reflections of Love

Look in the mirror, what do we see?
Two clowns in love, just wild and free.
Your funny faces ignite the whole room,
Together, we banish all traces of gloom.

In this funhouse of emotions, we play,
Riddles and laughter light up our day.
With quirks and laughs, we dance like kids,
In this silly love, nobody hides.

In the Space Between Us

You steal my snacks, I roll my eyes,
But deep inside, I know you're wise.
You snort while laughing, I nearly choke,
In our goofy world, it's all a joke.

Juggling pizza and bad dance moves,
You trip and fall, but still, you groove.
We're quite the pair, a funny sight,
Together we shine, so very bright.

Pulses Intertwined

You sing off-key in the shower stall,
I clap along, but I can't recall.
Your silly faces make me grin wide,
In this silly life, we take a ride.

We race with spoons and a bowl of peas,
Let's spill some juice and call it a tease.
In this quirky dance, we've made it clear,
Laughter is better when you're near.

Whispers of Connection

You kept my pen, it's gone for days,
But now you write in your funny ways.
With doodles of cats and a dog in shades,
Our thoughts align, like lemonade parades.

We whisper secrets while wearing hats,
Creating tales of swanky spats.
So here's to us, the jesters of fate,
Our goofy journey, I celebrate!

Rhythms of Togetherness

You made a mess with whipped cream pie,
We giggled hard, couldn't deny.
Our silly battles, they make the day,
In this wacky life, let's laugh and play.

With dancing socks and mismatched shoes,
We create chaos; it's hard to lose.
So let's keep spinning, round and round,
In our funny world, joy is found.

Luminescence in the Dark

In the night, you shine so bright,
Like a glowstick in a fright.
Your laughter echoes through the hall,
It lights up every wall.

With your quirks, you dance and twirl,
Like a cat in a dizzy whirl.
You trip on air, a comic show,
Our giggles form a lovely glow.

Tides of Affinity

We wave like beaches kissed by brine,
Your antics and jokes always just fine.
You splash around, cause a big scene,
Making waves like you're a marine.

At high tide, we laugh till we ache,
Our jokes like surfboards, we ride the wake.
A tidal pull that won't let go,
In playful waters, we both flow.

Unvoiced Promises

In silence, we swap silly grins,
With just a glance, our fun begins.
A wink here, a nod there,
A secret world, floating in air.

We don't need words, just our flair,
Like a mime in a café chair.
With each punchline and silly jest,
We link our hearts, put humor to the test.

Mosaics of Meaning

Our friendship's a patchwork, bright and bold,
Stitched with laughter, never cold.
Every piece tells a funny tale,
Like a treasure map with a quirky trail.

From mishaps to inside jokes we find,
A quilt of moments, perfectly designed.
In this mosaic, laughter is art,
A masterpiece that warms the heart.

Portraits of Joy

In a gallery of grins, we pose,
Mismatched socks and silly clothes.
Laughter hangs like silly art,
Captured smiles, a work of heart.

Each picture tells a funny tale,
Of chocolate spills and playful fail.
Silly faces, eyes askew,
A masterpiece of me and you.

A Journey Without Distance

We travel far without a map,
Idiot GPS in a comedy cap.
Lost in giggles, maps askew,
Finding joy is what we do.

No need for baggage, just some cheer,
A ticklish journey, bring good beer.
With every chuckle, the miles shrink,
Overflows of joy, never think!

Echoes of Our Beats

When you laugh, I join the sound,
Our giggles, echoes all around.
In sync we dance, like clumsy fools,
Waltzing by unwritten rules.

Heartfelt rhythms, beats entwined,
A symphony of the silly kind.
Tapping toes and goofy grins,
The song of us, where fun begins.

Two Souls Entwined

We tie our shoes and trip in sync,
Falling forward, we stop to think.
Who needs grace when we've got glee,
Two silly souls, just you and me.

In the dance of life, we sway,
Bumps and giggles lead the way.
With eyes wide shut, we spin around,
In our own circus, joy is found.

A Dance of Two Hearts

When you twirl, I trip and fall,
Your laugh bursts, echoing the hall.
We step on toes, but it's alright,
In our little dance, we take flight.

You lead with flair, I stumble behind,
In this rhythm, our joy we find.
With every turn, the crowd goes wild,
Our clumsy love, forever styled.

Serendipity's Embrace

A chance encounter at the café,
Where sugar spills, it's quite the display.
You ordered coffee, ended with tea,
Together we laugh, oh what a spree!

With muffins flying from your plate,
You blink, confused— isn't this fate?
Our clumsy fate, a buttered mix,
This happy mess, is quite the fix.

Heartstrings in Melody

You play a tune, I sing off-key,
The dog howls loud—what harmony!
With every note, a silly grin,
Our concert starts, let the fun begin!

In this duet, no perfection found,
But laughter rings, we spin around.
The notes may clash, but who could care?
In this sweet chaos, love fills the air.

A Symphony of Us

Two different rhythms, side by side,
You steal the show, I take the ride.
With each messy beat, we find delight,
What a circus act, oh what a sight!

Your kazoo playing, my tambourine,
Together we make quite the scene.
In this symphony, laughter swells,
Our quirky tune, the world compels.

The Weight of Presence

When you're around, my socks feel tight,
Your laugh's a feather, but oh, what a sight!
We ponder life, while munching on fries,
Your wisdom's gold, your jokes are the prize.

You trip on air, I snort my drink,
In our crazy dance, we seldom think.
Two clowns in a circus, bright as the day,
Together we tumble, in this goofy ballet.

A Sea of Emotions

A wave of laughter, here comes a splash,
Your silly faces make my heart dash.
We sail on puns, through stormy delight,
With every quip, the world feels just right.

Each joke's a boat, we joyfully row,
In this ocean of fun, we let our hearts flow.
Your wink is a buoy, bobbing on high,
Navigating chuckles 'neath a bright, silly sky.

The Symphony of Being

In this concert hall of whispers and cheer,
We play our minds; the melody's clear.
Your banter's the beat, my jokes are the tune,
Together we strum under a silly moon.

Drumroll of giggles, a symphonic burst,
This playful sonata quenches our thirst.
With each lifted brow, the laughter ignites,
A rhythm of joy, the best of delights.

Connection's Lullaby

Late-night talks, with cookies galore,
Your wild imagination, I always adore.
With dreams so whacky, we float to the moon,
In our cozy corner, no room for gloom.

Your stories tickle, like feathers on skin,
Together we giggle, let the fun begin.
With each shared secret, we craft a sweet song,
In this lullaby world, where we both belong.

Rhythms of Our Souls

When you dance, I trip and fall,
Your laughter echoes, a joyful call.
We spin in circles, round and round,
In this silly waltz, true love is found.

Your quirks make me giggle and sigh,
Like your weird obsession with fried pie.
Together we make a clumsy pair,
Yet in this chaos, there's love everywhere.

We both sing out of tune, quite a sight,
But in our laughter, the world feels right.
Chocolate smeared on your cheek like a crown,
You're the king of fun in this goofy town.

Our souls are a melody, offbeat and sweet,
Two eccentric rhythms, a shuffled heartbeat.
With every laugh, our spirits unite,
Dancing in humor, under the moonlight.

Echoes in Euphoria

With each joke, you lighten my load,
You tell tales of squirrels, on their crazy road.
Your puns hit harder than a shoe on a toe,
Yet in this laughter, my fondness does grow.

You steal my fries, and I give you the eye,
But those stolen bites are the sweetest of pie.
In our goofy games, we find joy anew,
A silly duet, just me and you.

Our giggles echo in the quiet night,
Every glance exchanged feels just so right.
You dance like a chicken, I jump like a frog,
In this frolicsome world, you're my favorite hog.

In our absurdity, bliss is concealed,
Together we laugh, our fate is revealed.
No matter the chaos, I know we won't part,
For in all the madness, you have my whole heart.

Threads of Tenderness

Your socks, mismatched, are a sight to behold,
Like a closet explosion of colors untold.
You wear that grin like it's your best tee,
Each chuckle we share hooks my heart like a flea.

You sing in the shower, it drives me insane,
But those off-key notes are my favorite refrain.
With each goofy glance, my day lights up bright,
In your silly world, I find pure delight.

We share inside jokes, only we can recall,
Like dancing with llamas at a festival ball.
Your quirks are the threads that stitch love so tight,
In this tapestry woven, everything's right.

Though life may be messy, with spills on the floor,
Your laughter's a treasure, I simply adore.
Our hearts are knitted in this fabric divine,
Amidst all the humor, your hand's still in mine.

Embraces Beyond Time

In this goofy dance, we lose track of days,
With laughter and sprinkles, we're lost in a maze.
Time doesn't matter when we're having fun,
Chasing after sunsets, or a runaway bun.

You attempt magic tricks, but they always flop,
Yet your hopeful grin makes my heart just stop.
With every misstep, we just can't get bored,
In this playful scheme, there's love to be scored.

Cuddling up close, wrapped tight like a gift,
Your tickles and whispers send me on a lift.
We'll race flying clouds on this whimsical ride,
And hold onto love like a wild roller tide.

So let's sprinkle joy on each day we embrace,
With puns and with laughter, we'll dance through the race.
In the winks of forever, where laughter aligns,
Our hearts beat together, in whimsical times.

Resonating Echoes

In the hall of chatterboxes,
Two beats play a game of toss.
One goes left, the other right,
Like socks that dance in lazy light.

With every bounce, we share a laugh,
A symphony of silly gaffes.
Echoes ring from wall to wall,
As we trip and stumble, then have a ball.

Our giggles bounce like rubber bands,
In perfect time with silly hands.
A tickle here, a poke right there,
Creating music in the air.

So when the rhythm starts to sway,
Join the jam, don't fade away.
In this wacky, joyous place,
We make a tune, a funny space.

A Journey in Sync

Two quirky hearts on a bus ride,
Joking on the bumpy side.
Laugh lines stretch, a sight to see,
As we bickering over who's got the key.

With snacks that fly like carefree birds,
And laughter louder than any words.
Every turn's a chance to tease,
While the universe giggles, too, with ease.

We twirl around and take a chance,
In a waltz of wobble, a silly dance.
Through life's chaos, we find our spark,
Navigating trails through light and dark.

Our journey's filled with ups and downs,
Like riding roller coasters in silly crowns.
Side by side, we scribble our tale,
In a slightly mad, colorful trail.

The Space Between Beats

In the rhythm of our playful race,
You step on my toes, I laugh and brace.
The gap between our silly beats,
Fills with laughter, where fun repeats.

In the pauses, we toss each line,
Like juggling balls of wittiness divine.
Your grin's a Bell that plays my tune,
As we two-step beneath the moon.

Every giggle adds a pop,
In this dance, we cannot stop.
With a twist and twirl, we find our place,
In this funny, funky space.

The space between our heartbeats sways,
Creating jokes in playful ways.
In the joy of chaos, we stay aligned,
In the quirky, crazy connects we find.

Affection's Map

We draw a map with crayons bright,
Of giggles shared in morning light.
Every tickle leads to trails,
Of silly faces and jokey tales.

X marks the spot where laughter blooms,
In the land of puns and goofy rooms.
With every step, we chart our course,
Like a rollercoaster of feline force.

Navigating through heart-shaped lanes,
Where chuckles turn into silly gains.
At the crossroads of belly laughs,
We rewrite the world on paper drafts.

So take my hand, let's stroll afar,
In this map of love, we know where we are.
Through the land of jest and cheer,
We'll be best friends, year after year.

The Firefly Connection

In the garden we dance around,
Chasing bugs that make no sound.
I swear they wink, you'd think they tease,
Yet we both trip and land with ease.

You giggle with that goofy grin,
As fireflies buzz on a whim.
We leap and spin, it's quite a sight,
Two clumsy fools in the summer light.

With jars in hand, we try our luck,
To catch the glow, but we're out of luck.
These little lights just laugh and fly,
While we grow weary, oh my, oh my!

So let's abandon this firefly chase,
And find more fun in our silly space.
Perhaps a dance or a pie to bake,
Because even bugs know how to partake.

The Lighthouse of Our Bond

On cliffs so high, we spot the beam,
It flashes bright like our shared dream.
A lighthouse guides with steadfast light,
While we fumble through our playful night.

You bump your head on the narrow door,
I laugh so hard, I roll on the floor.
In this silly place, we chuckle loud,
Echoing joy that makes us proud.

We trade our snacks, a pie for fries,
Your dream of pizza, oh what a surprise!
We toast with sodas in glittery cups,
While the lighthouse beams, it fully erupts.

As the tide swooshes in with a roar,
We count the seagulls, then count some more.
Two spirits lost in laughter's embrace,
Forever anchored in this strange place.

Fragmented Wholeness

In pieces we laugh, a puzzle undone,
You're a corner, I'm part of the fun.
With odd shapes tangled, we fit quite right,
Who knew chaos could spark such delight?

As you try to fit my little piece,
You poke yourself, oh what a tease!
Yet we giggle as we don't quite align,
The best mismatched pairs are surely divine.

Together we paint our clumsy art,
With colors splashed, a giggly heart.
Who needs a pattern or sense of tame,
In this wildness, we find our name.

Let's scribble more, a masterpiece rare,
With hands all messy, no time to spare.
Fragmented we stand, yet whole like the sea,
In this chaos, you'll always find me.

Between the Lines of Us

In the margins, we scribble dreams,
With doodles and jokes, or so it seems.
You draw a cat, I sketch a dog,
Our paper-bound stories in a fog.

We write our thoughts in twisty prose,
Where every pun and joke just flows.
You miss the line, it's just too funny,
I choke on laughter, sweet like honey.

Between the letters, a world is born,
Of giggles and snorts from the early morn.
Our jokes can't end, they twist and twine,
In this book of life, your hand in mine.

So let's write more in this crazy style,
Where laughter lives and humor's worthwhile.
Between our lines, the joy we share,
Is written in giggles, light as air.

Silent Promises

In whispers shared beneath the moon,
Two silly souls, not quite in tune.
You nod, I laugh, what's on your mind?
A secret pact, of laughter designed.

With every giggle, shadows dance,
Our hearts agree to take a chance.
A comedy of cues and blinks,
Silent vows in chalkboard inks.

As clouds drift by in playful glee,
We swap the stories, you and me.
In jest we promise, oh so bright,
To keep each other laughing all night.

Heartbeats at Dusk

As daylight slips, we start to play,
With beat in sync, we dance away.
A tap, a skip, a silly twirl,
Life's a jest, oh what a whirl!

Your left foot fumbles, mine gets stuck,
Yet in this mess, we find our luck.
Our laughter rings, a joyful sound,
In evening's glow, pure happiness found.

Racing shadows, quick on our feet,
In this strange ballet, we can't be beat.
With every tick, we steal the show,
Two clowns lost, just letting it flow.

Unity in Duality

Two peas in a pod, so strange, so fine,
Dancing around in a zany line.
You say it's weird, I nod with glee,
Together, we're quite the sight to see!

Your quirk is charming, mine's a tease,
In this circus, we aim to please.
Balancing acts on life's great stage,
Together we giggle—let's turn the page!

In playful banter, we find our sway,
Like mismatched socks on laundry day.
A duo unique, a perfect blend,
Through laughter and fun, we'll never end.

The Pulse of Together

In a world of rhythm, we find our beat,
Two hearts collide, oh what a feat!
A wacky march, we're out of sync,
Yet in this madness, we find our link.

With every chuckle, the tempo climbs,
Turning everyday into silly rhymes.
Shuffling feet in a goofy dance,
Eager grins, we take a chance.

Through bursts of joy, our spirits rise,
A spectacle spun under starry skies.
In pulses shared, it's clear to see,
Life's a comedy for you and me!

Mosaic of Togetherness

In the bakery of life, we mix our dough,
Adding sprinkles of laughter, making it glow.
You knead the quirks, I roll with the fun,
Together we're baking, under the sun.

Like mismatched socks, we dance and we twirl,
Swapping our hiccups, giving it a whirl.
Your giggle's the icing, my chuckles the cake,
In the mosaic of moments, it's fun that we make.

On Mondays, you snore, while I sip my tea,
In our home of oddities, we're all we can be.
With goofy grins pasted, we conquer the day,
In our quirky little world, we find our way.

Through the puzzle of chaos, we fit just right,
A sitcom of misfits, in day and in night.
We laugh at the mess, with noodles on the floor,
Mosaic of togetherness, who could want more?

Footprints in the Heart

We stomp around puddles, splashes and squeals,
Leaving muddy tales that laughter reveals.
Each footprint a memory, as silly as bread,
Tracing our journeys, where giggles are spread.

Like socks on a hamster, we wiggle and sway,
Chasing the clouds that decide to play.
With whimsy as our guide, we sometimes trip too,
But the footprints we leave, are what make us, us two.

In a wacky parade, of mismatched delight,
Even our shadows are having a fright.
We stumble, we tumble, but oh what a art,
These footprints of love, are stamped on our heart.

So here's to the laughter, and all that we share,
With footprints of joy that dance through the air.
In puddles of giggles, we leave our mark,
A trail of pure laughter, brightening the dark.

Unison in Quietude

In the quiet of mornings, you steal all the toast,
While I dream of bacon, oh you silly ghost.
With coffee in hand, and crumbs on the floor,
We giggle and snicker, what's life without more?

In comfortable silence, we borrow each space,
Two peas in a pod, with crumbs on our face.
As the world starts to buzz, we savor the calm,
Like koalas in trees, we wrap in our charm.

Your socks in the fridge? Now that's quite a laugh,
Together we chuckle, it's love on our path.
We sip on our tea, and snicker with glee,
In moments of quiet, you're right here with me.

Though mischief may beckon and chaos may reign,
In unison of calm, there's joy in the mundane.
With whispers and winks, our hearts find the tune,
In the melody of silence, we dance to our rune.

Dreamscapes of Affection

In the land of our dreams, where giggles grow tall,
We bounce on soft clouds, and giggle and fall.
With unicorns winking, we dance on the moon,
In dreamscapes of joy, we're never immune.

The stars wear our shenanigans, twinkling with pride,
As we hiccup and snort, on this magical ride.
Your silly snorts echo, like cannonballs blast,
In our blissful adventure, we're having a blast.

From marshmallow rivers, to castles of cheese,
We're kings of the chaos, living with ease.
You trip on a dragon, and both start to squeal,
In dreamscapes of laughter, we find what is real.

So let's build a fortress with pillows and dreams,
Where laughter and fun flow like colorful streams.
In this land of enchantment, we'll sparkle and play,
Through dreamscapes of affection, forever we'll stay.

The Fire We Share

In a world of warmth and spice,
Your laugh ignites my inner vice.
Burning marshmallows, oh so sweet,
Our silly dances, can't be beat.

With every giggle, flames do soar,
We throw on jokes, who could ask for more?
S'mores of laughter, a crunchy delight,
As we roast our dreams beneath the night.

We trot like ducks, a goofy parade,
In this bonfire, memories made.
Your silly faces, my heart's delight,
Together sparking, a joyful flight.

So let's stoke the spark with a wink,
In this carnival, our spirits sink.
With playful banter, hearts will glow,
In the fire we share, let love overflow.

Merging Currents

Two rivers meet, a twisty flow,
You splash and giggle, where shall we go?
Water balloon fights, oh what a mess,
We swim like fish, in our funny dress.

With rubber ducks in brave display,
We paddle through life, come what may.
Drifting on laughter, a silly spree,
In waves of joy, just you and me.

A tidal wave of memes to share,
Your quirky stories fill the air.
Cannonballs splash, with woeful grace,
We laugh 'til we snort, what a race!

As ebb meets flow, our fates collide,
In this ocean of giggles, let's take a ride.
Together we'll sail, through day and night,
In this merging dance, life feels so right.

In the Heart's Embrace

Two puzzle pieces, fit so snug,
We cuddle closely, oh what a mug!
Your goofy grin, a sight to see,
In this cozy nook, just you and me.

Adventures await in this funny place,
As we waltz through life, in a silly race.
Tickle fights and silly pranks,
Create a treasure trove of thanks.

We've got inside jokes, a secret code,
With laughter echoing down each road.
When life gets dull, we turn the page,
A banquet of mirth, at every stage.

So here's our tale of laughter sweet,
In the heart's embrace, life's dance complete.
With every giggle and wink we share,
In this cozy nook, there's joy in the air.

Constellations of Connection

Under the starlight, we spin and sway,
Creating a show, in a silly way.
Your cosmic giggles light up the dark,
Outrageous dances, leave a mark.

In a galaxy filled with laughter bright,
We chase the moons, like stars in flight.
Satellite snacks, pop and crunch,
As we float on dreams, in a wild bunch.

Through constellations, we draw our map,
In a zany world, we take a nap.
With rubber aliens, and capes galore,
We travel through the cosmos, forever more.

So here's to the stars, our endless quest,
In this wacky dance, we are truly blessed.
With a burst of laughter, we light up the night,
In constellations of connection, everything feels right.

The Canvas of Together

We painted dreams in hues of lime,
In a room that smelled of toasted thyme.
You spilled the paint right on my nose,
I laughed so hard, I struck a pose.

A masterpiece of silly art,
With every blob, you stole my heart.
Your brushstrokes dance, they flip and twirl,
I'm here for giggles, my silly girl.

Two mismatched socks on the kitchen floor,
You claim it's fashion, but I'm not sure.
When you skip and trip, it's quite a sight,
In our canvas world, everything feels right.

So let's mix colors in our quirky way,
In this gallery of laugh-filled play.
With every mess, I'll raise a toast,
To the joyful art we love the most.

Beneath Shared Skies

Underneath the wobbly moon,
We danced and sang a silly tune.
You stepped on toes, a clumsy show,
But I just laughed, you steal the show.

The stars above were piscatorial,
We named the clouds as if themorial.
With coffee cups, we mapped the sky,
You tried to fly, oh my oh my!

In puddles deep, our laughter shines,
You made a splash with buttered lines.
We giggled at the silly sights,
As thunder played the drum of nights.

So here's to nights of wishes bright,
Beneath the skies that feel just right.
With you beside, the world's a glee,
Who knew love could be so quirky?

Echoing Emotions

With every echo, a giggle's tossed,
In a valley of laughter, we both are lost.
I shout your name, it springs back clear,
You toss a snack, and we both cheer.

The walls might hear our joking din,
As we play tags, and we both spin.
You prance around, a silly dance,
Look at our joy, it's quite the chance!

Through echoing rooms of jumbled fun,
We laugh till tears, the day undone.
With each note laughed, a heartfelt cheer,
I'm glad you're close, let's keep you near.

In this symphony of love and jest,
With booming laughs, we're truly blessed.
So let's make noise, oh what a treat,
In echoing joy, our hearts do meet.

Tidal Waves of Affection

On the shore, with sand on toes,
You built a castle, then it froze!
A wave came crashing, kings and queens,
We laughed so hard, forgot the scenes.

The ocean's giggle, a playful roar,
You named the fish, let's add one more!
With every splash, a memory made,
In our sea of fun, we wade and fade.

Seaweed crowns, we wore them proud,
With every chuckle, we drew a crowd.
Your joyful shouts, a siren's call,
With you beside, I'd choose it all.

So let the tidal waves of cheer,
Carry our hearts through laughter's sphere.
In this ocean, let's make a splash,
With each silly wave, together we dash.

The Ties We Weave

In the garden where laughter blooms,
We trip on vines and dodge the brooms.
Two tangled souls with socks askew,
Like mismatched shoes, we fit askew.

The spaghetti dance, a messy twirl,
We laugh so hard, our faces whirl.
Your elbow nudges, my drink goes wide,
In this chaotic joy, we abide.

With silly jokes and puppy eyes,
We spin our tales, watch time fly by.
A hiccup here, a snort out there,
Our hearts sync up, a quirky pair.

And oh, the quirks that make us laugh,
Like puzzle pieces, we find our path.
In every giggle, in every tease,
Together, we dance in perfect ease.

Untold Feelings

There's a secret language in our sighs,
Like baked potatoes that wear disguise.
Underneath the laughter, a wink, a grin,
A mystery like where socks have been.

A bucket of fries and double dip,
You cackle loud, I take a sip.
Hidden messages in every bite,
Like ice cream sundaes under starlight.

With every giggle, a feeling grows,
Like a rubber band that never slows.
The teasing jabs and playful shoves,
Hint at a thousand silly loves.

We share the truth wrapped all in jest,
With every chuckle, we're truly blessed.
In every punchline, there's something more,
Untold feelings at the core.

Colliding Universes

Your planet spins with silly dreams,
While I orbit 'round chocolate streams.
When we collide, it's pure delight,
Like stars that dance on Saturday night.

Through cosmic laughter, we twist and glide,
Bright meteors in a twisted ride.
We bounce like comets, bright and bold,
Our goofy tales are pure gold.

Two galaxies in a tangled race,
With every laugh, we find our place.
A starship fueled by joy and fun,
Orbiting circles until we're done.

In this space where giggles reign,
Our worlds combine, a cosmic chain.
With every chuckle, we stand apart,
Yet merge in harmony, two worlds, one heart.

The Beat of Belonging

In the rhythm of laughter, we find our beats,
Like socks with stripes and tasty sweets.
We shimmy and shake with silly grace,
In this goofy dance, we've found our place.

Your jokes, a melody that makes me grin,
Like mixing up the blues and skin.
We hop like frogs, and clown around,
In the laughter, our love is found.

Beatboxing hearts, a two-step spree,
With every hiccup, we're wild and free.
Laughter's the tune, we're dancing along,
In the song of silly, we truly belong.

Like pairs of shoes that never part,
In every chuckle, you've won my heart.
Together we trumpet, we're funny, we're bold,
In the rhythm of belonging, love unfolds.

A Journey of Echoes

In a land of giggles and loud cheer,
Voices bounce back, oh so near.
We take steps, then trip with flair,
Laughter dances in the air.

Each pun we toss, a playful dart,
Silly faces, a work of art.
With every joke, we lose control,
Together, we make each other whole.

Echoes of chaos fill the space,
A symphony of smiles on each face.
We leap from thoughts to a better joke,
In this journey, we never choke.

In this wild ride, we just can't hide,
From the mischief our hearts provide.
Through the ups and downs, we fly so free,
In this laughter, it's just you and me.

Starlit Conversations

Under stars, we laugh out loud,
We share our secrets, a silly crowd.
With jellybeans and silly chats,
We ponder life with goofy hats.

What if trees could wear a tie?
Or if cows could dance and fly?
With every tale, we twist and twirl,
Each whimsy thought makes our heads swirl.

Our voices blend like a sweet song,
In this madness, how can it be wrong?
The cosmos giggles, a friendly host,
Shooting stars join in, we're not a ghost.

As we ponder what dreams may come,
The universe smiles, tapping a drum.
With each chuckle, the night ignites,
In starlit chats, our hearts take flight.

The Embrace of Understanding

Wacky thoughts like pancakes stack,
In a world where logic seems to lack.
We share a smile, it's quite absurd,
With every nod, it feels like the third.

When I'm lost, you humor my plight,
With puns and jokes that feel so right.
You decipher my quirks like a code,
Our friendship runs down a merry road.

In the dance of goof and grace,
We embrace the odd, this quirky space.
With laughter's warmth, we weave a quilt,
In the threads of giggles, love is built.

So here we stand, in this delight,
Enemies of boredom, stars burn bright.
Through fun and antics, we understand,
In this embrace, we make our stand.

Memory Lane of Us

Down memory lane, we skip and hop,
Every silly moment, we can't stop.
Like clowns in a circus, we play our part,
Painting the world with a laughing heart.

From dancing squirrels to flying pies,
Laughter bubbles, oh what a surprise!
Flipped pancakes on ceilings, what a sight,
We giggle 'til dawn, it feels so right.

Our scrapbook's filled with chaos and cheer,
With every picture, the laughter's near.
Funny faces, and blunders galore,
Together, we craft forevermore.

So here's to us, the jesters we be,
In this hilarity, we're so carefree.
Through memory lanes, we'll forever roam,
In giggles and smiles, we find our home.

Bridges of Hope

In a world where sock puppets dance,
We build our paths with silly chance.
From your giggle to my silly grin,
Together we find where fun begins.

Each step we take, a hop, a skip,
With wobbly knees and ice cream drip.
We chase our dreams on roller skates,
Laughing at all the odd debates.

Unicorns wear shades and ride bikes,
While our laughter sparks the funniest hikes.
Through puddles we splash, painting the air,
Crafting joy from the little we share.

With every joke, a bridge we lay,
Connecting hearts in the silliest way.
So grab my hand, let's jump and twirl,
Together we'll dance, oh, what a whirl!

The Warmth of Interlaced Hands

Two hands tangled in a funny fight,
Like spaghetti and meatballs on a plate at night.
We wrestle like kittens, giggling away,
As warmth spreads through, come what may.

Fingers entwined, we form a knot,
A silly bond, a joyful spot.
In moments shared, we play our part,
Turning clumsy gestures into art.

Like a pair of socks lost in the wash,
We find our rhythm, a laugh or gaffe.
With every squeeze, the world's less bland,
Together we stand, a mismatched band.

In this dance, we find our place,
Creating joy with each embrace.
Through snickers and snorts, the love expands,
In this crazy life, we hold our hands.

Secrets in the Silence

In the quiet, we share our quirks,
Like clumsy dance moves and silly smirks.
An awkward shrug, a knowing glance,
In this hush, we take our chance.

With eyebrows raised, we play charades,
Giggles bubbling behind the shades.
Our thoughts float by on silent streams,
Turning whispers into wild dreams.

The secrets bloom in a sideways glance,
Inside jokes that lead to a dance.
Laughter hides where silence sleeps,
In the blend of hearts, joy gently creeps.

Each pause we take is a playful tease,
Building stories with the greatest ease.
So here we sit, in quiet delight,
Crafting fun while the world's out of sight.

Kindred Spirits' Flame

In a castle made of pillows tall,
We battle dragons, we will not fall.
With marshmallow swords, we take our stand,
Laughing together, side by side we'll land.

Our spirits dance like flames that twirl,
Spinning stories in a whimsical whirl.
Each flicker a memory, bright and clear,
Creating warmth filled with cheer.

With shadows cast from candlelight,
We turn our giggles into flight.
The night is young, our hearts are free,
In this playful land, just you and me.

We'll chase the stars with our grinning faces,
Finding joy in the silliest places.
So throw your hand in mine, my friend,
Together we'll laugh till the very end.

Chemistries of the Heart

In a lab of love, we mix and pour,
With giggles and chuckles, who could want more?
Silly reactions, like soda in socks,
Fizzing and popping, oh what a paradox!

Your smile's a catalyst, igniting the fun,
With every quirk, our bond's never done.
Molecules dancing, a frolicsome chase,
In this mad experiment, we find our place.

A Fusion of Feelings

Bananas and pickles, a combo bizarre,
Yet here we are, a radiant star.
Mixing our flavors, odd as they seem,
In our kitchen of laughter, we whip up a dream.

Swapping the recipes, you bake me a cake,
With sprinkles of chaos, oh for goodness' sake!
Our taste buds collide, fusion gourmet,
In this feast of delight, let's dance the day away.

Wanderers in Harmony

Two lost socks in a drawer full of space,
Together we wander, never a trace.
With maps made of giggles, we roam far and wide,
In our little adventure, there's no need to hide.

Chasing the rainbows and puddles of joy,
We stumble on pathways, oh what a ploy!
In the circus of life, we juggle and tease,
As wanderers together, we do it with ease.

Our Unwritten Sonnet

In the book of our lives, pages blank and free,
We scribble with laughter, you and me.
Silly rhymes tumble like leaves in the breeze,
Each line is a smile, as light as you please.

With no need for structure, just rhythm and flow,
Imperfect perfection, that's how we go.
So let's write our story with joy and a dart,
In the comical chapters, you play my part.

Shadows of Togetherness

In the park, we dance and twirl,
Dodging squirrels and laughing girls.
You trip, I giggle, we lose our cool,
Together we're the funniest fools.

A shared ice cream, melting fast,
You take a lick, it's gone at last.
We both wear chocolate on our face,
A sweet disaster, a silly race.

Your jokes are bad, but I don't mind,
Laughter's magic, it's so divine.
We fall in fits when your punchlines flop,
In this silly duo, fun just won't stop.

Like shadows cast in the evening sun,
Two haunted hearts, we joke and run.
With every laugh, our spirits soar,
Together always, who could ask for more?

The Pulse of Affection

You steal my fries, I steal a bite,
We share our food, a tasty plight.
With every nibble, we laugh and scheme,
Life's absurdity is quite the dream.

Your fashion sense—oh what a sight,
Stripes and polka dots clash outright.
Yet with you, I wear my quirkiest gear,
We march like peacocks, full of cheer.

Every prank we pull is full of glee,
Like whoopee cushions on a three-legged bee.
Our laughter echoes, a quirky sound,
In this little world, we're tightly bound.

With quirky heartbeats matching fast,
Life's a comedy, a hoot, a blast.
Let's step through puddles, make a mess,
Together we thrive, in pure happiness.

A Tapestry of Touch

Your handshake's firm, but watch out, please,
A tickle here, or a pinch with ease.
We tackle life with such silly grace,
Like two balloon animals in a race.

Our high-fives often miss the mark,
A swing and a miss, well, it's our spark.
With every attempt that goes amiss,
We share a laugh, it's pure bliss.

Fingers intertwined like spaghetti strands,
Messy and jumbled, but surely planned.
We craft our bond, in playful might,
Joking 'til sunset, we warm the night.

Through pats and nudges, we build our tale,
A tapestry woven with giggly fail.
Every moment a stitch, woven tight,
In this grand quilt of pure delight.

Boundless Echoes

In crowded rooms, you strike a pose,
A goofy grin, and everyone knows.
Your dance moves set the floor ablaze,
We steal the spotlight, a laugh-filled craze.

Whispers shared over too much cake,
You drop a slice, make no mistake.
We both erupt, a sweet delight,
In this mishap, we light the night.

Like rubber bands, we stretch and pull,
Silly faces, our hearts are full.
We flip and flop, like a rubber duck,
In this grand chase, we've got the luck.

Each echo of laughter fills the air,
A boundless joy, beyond compare.
In every giggle, our spirits blend,
Together forever, we'll always send.

Unfurling Together

In a garden where laughter blooms,
We tickle each other with silly riddles.
You hide the snacks, I find the spoons,
Together we dance, dodging the giggles.

A race for the cookies becomes a showdown,
You trip on my shoelace, what a flip!
With flour on our noses, we sit on the crown,
In this chaos, we share the best trip.

Butterflies flutter, confetti falls,
The world spins wildly, who knew?
We tie our shoelaces, hear the calls,
Of friends who giggle at our to-and-fro.

In a tapestry woven of silly things,
We bounce on clouds made of marshmallow.
Life's a circus while the laughter sings,
In our fun house, there's always a shadow.

A Garden of Shared Dreams

In a meadow where daisies wink,
We plant our hopes in pots of gold.
With rubber boots and socks in sync,
Giggling wildly, we break the mold.

Watering cans held like trophies high,
Each drop spills secrets, oh such fun!
We're two crazy gardeners, oh my!
Sunburned smiles, our work's not done.

We chase the butterflies in the sun,
With jars for dreams and a squeaky wheel.
In our patch where wild antics run,
Every flicker of joy feels surreal.

Roses laugh, their thorns do prance,
As we twirl like weeds in a breeze.
In our garden of quirky romance,
Every petal invites us to seize.

Threads of Intimacy

Stitching moments with a playful thread,
We knot our laughs in homemade quilts.
Your antics huge, my jokes widespread,
In this patchwork, joy is built.

Needles flying like a frantic crew,
With mismatched colors, our laughter blends.
We embroider stories, just us two,
In this tapestry where silliness extends.

Buttons pop off with each hearty chuckle,
Patterns of fun spin out of control.
We mend the seams of every snuggle,
Crafting joy on this shared stroll.

Snips of joy scatter, can you believe?
Our imaginary scissors clip away.
Together we weave what we both conceive,
In this dance of delight, we sway.

Crescendo of Compassion

In a symphony of hiccups and snorts,
Our hearts play tunes that make all laugh.
With every note, our mischief resorts,
To creating a band from a silly gaff.

You strum the air with exaggerated flair,
I drop the tambourine, what a sound!
Our laughter echoes, filling the air,
In this concerto where fun is found.

We march like penguins, united in song,
Each beat a joke, no step goes right.
A funny parade, where we both belong,
In this melody, we shine so bright.

With drumsticks made from carrots and glee,
We tap our toes in perfect rhythm.
Compassion crescendos in harmony,
As we sway through life's funny prism.

Celestial Rhythms

In the sky, our laughter twirls,
Like disco balls with tiny pearls.
Stars wink and giggle in delight,
As we dance through the cosmic night.

Comets zoom with hilarious flair,
Tickling the moon without a care.
Constellations cheer in a row,
As we whirl in this cosmic show.

The planets hum a silly tune,
Jupiter swims, while Mars just croons.
We bounce on clouds, all fluffy and bright,
Creating joy in this starry flight.

With every twist, we laugh and spin,
Around the sun, let the fun begin!
In this universe of goofy cheer,
We're the stars that shine so clear.

Gold Threads of Warmth

In a quilt of giggles, we are sewn,
Patches of joy, brightly blown.
Warming up in every stitch,
Life's a comedy, not a hitch.

Sunshine threads, with laughter intertwined,
Every snicker perfectly aligned.
We wrap ourselves in cozy glee,
A tapestry of hilarity.

In every fold, a joke unfolds,
Stories of warmth that never gets old.
Like a golden hug that warms the soul,
Our spirits bounce, we're on a roll.

As we snuggle tight in this fun-filled nest,
Life's a best friend, just like the rest.
Let's stitch this giggle to the seams,
In a quilt of warmth, full of dreams.

The Fabric of Us

Two threads woven, side by side,
In a fabric where quirks reside.
With every laugh, we loom and weave,
A playful patchwork, hard to believe.

Checkered smiles, polka-dots of cheer,
Sewing together with threads so dear.
Every snicker, a seam most divine,
As we jump into the fabric line.

Our quirky patterns can't help but show,
A rainbow of giggles, a vibrant glow.
Every fold brings a burst of fun,
In the fabric of us, we've already won.

With a twist and a turn, we create a spree,
A canvas of laughter, just you and me.
We dance through colors, stitch it all tight,
In this fabric of friendship, pure delight!

Interlaced Souls

Together we blend like a curious stew,
Whisking up laughter, just me and you.
With a spoonful of jokes and a dash of fun,
Our interlaced souls can't be outdone.

We bubble and giggle, let out a cheer,
Mixing our quirks, the silliness clear.
A pinch of chaos and a sprinkle of grace,
In this crazy pot, we find our place.

Sailing on waves of zany delight,
Our shared laughter ignites the night.
Like two silly fish in the sea of fate,
Together we swim, never too late.

As we stir up the joy with each little twist,
This interlaced bond is hard to resist.
In our chuckling journey, we both take part,
As we dance through life, entwined at heart.

Heartfelt Bridges

When you snore like a giant bear,
I wonder if you know it's not fair.
Yet cuddling in blankets so tight,
We giggle 'til morning light.

You stole my fries, I stole your hat,
In this playful game, we both sat.
With laughter flying in every direction,
Our love is a funny connection.

In silly dances, we both trip,
As we munch on popcorn, we never skip.
Every hiccup just makes us roar,
Who knew this love could be such a chore!

Together we stumble, we laugh, we trip,
Navigating life on a comical ship.
So here's to our whims, wild and free,
The fun we create is just you and me.

The Garden of Us

In a garden where laughter blooms wide,
You tell the best jokes, I can't hide.
Petunias giggle, and daisies sway,
We plant our dreams in a fun way.

You water the jokes, I tend to the puns,
Together we grow, two silly buns.
In the sunshine, we dance and play,
Turning mundane into a grand ballet.

Bees buzz to our silly tunes,
They know we light up the afternoons.
With every bloom, a smile is grown,
In this funny space, we feel at home.

So let's dig up some weeds of despair,
With laughter and joy, here's our flair.
In the garden of us, how we thrive,
Two goofballs making the world come alive.

Shades of Mutual Affection

In every shade of laughter's glee,
We paint our days, just you and me.
When you slip on a banana peel,
I laugh so hard, it's quite surreal.

Your funny faces make the world bright,
With every wink, you bring me delight.
In this quirky dance, we won't refrain,
Two comics in love, going insane.

We juggle life's lemons, sip lemonade,
In our amusement park, joy won't fade.
Through pranks and jokes, we find our way,
Crafting a bond that just wants to play.

Like a circus act, we leap and twist,
In this fun journey, we can't resist.
With every chuckle, our hearts align,
In this joyful mess, we brightly shine.

The Pulse of Understanding

In the rhythm of our silly chats,
We find beats like clumsy musical rats.
When you trip over air, my heart skips,
You bounce up with laughter, doing flips.

Every pun you throw is a joyous treat,
In this symphony, we find our beat.
With tickles and grins, we dance and sway,
Creating a melody that's here to stay.

Life's a joke, and we're the stars,
Sipping coffee and counting our scars.
In the notes of laughter, we share our song,
In this quirky duet, we both belong.

So let's strum the strings of wacky dreams,
In the pulse of life, laughter streams.
With every giggle and shared gaze,
We craft our symphony in silly ways.

www.ingramcontent.com/pod-product-compliance
Ingram Content Group UK Ltd.
Pitfield, Milton Keynes, MK11 3LW, UK
UKHW020126171224
452675UK00014BA/1605

9 789908 004839